Fiddle Time Runners

Piano accompaniment book

Kathy and David Blackwell

OXFORD
UNIVERSITY PRESS

OXFORD
UNIVERSITY PRESS

Great Clarendon Street, Oxford OX2 6DP,
United Kingdom

Cover illustration by Martin Remphry

Music and text origination by Katie Johnston and Julia Bovee
Printed in Great Britain

Contents

1. Start the show

KB & DB

2. Banyan tree

Jamaican folk tune

3. Heat haze

KB & DB

Relaxed

4. Medieval tale

KB & DB

5. Cornish May song

Cornish folk tune

6. Chase in the dark

KB & DB